Songs of the Cowboys
by N. Howard "Jack" Thorp

APPLEWOOD BOOKS

Songs of the Cowboys was originally
published by the author in 1908.

ISBN 1-55709-122-6

10 9 8 7 6 5

PREFACE

❧ ❧

To the Ranchmen of the West this little volume is dedicated as a reminder of the trail days and round-ups of the past. To the younger generation who know not of the trip from Texas to Dodge and the north, it will tend to keep alive the memories of an industry now past.

I have gathered these songs from the cow camps of different states and territories. They embrace most of the songs as sung by the oldtime cow punchers. I plead ignorant of the authorship of them but presume that most of the composers have, ere now, "Gone up the dim narrow trail."

I mount this little book on one of the best cow horses that ever lived, and start it on its journey; together may they meet all the old time cowboys and receive a welcome at their hands, is the earnest wish of

THE AUTHOR.

CONTENTS

❦ ❦

Songs of the Cowboys

Little Joe, the Wrangler

🌱 🌱 🌱

Little Joe, the wrangler, will never wrangle more;
　His days with the "Remuda"—they are done.
'Twas a year ago last April he joined the outfit here,
　A little "Texas Stray" and all alone.

'Twas long late in the evening he rode up to the herd
　On a little old brown pony he called Chaw;
With his brogan shoes and overalls a harder looking kid
　You never in your life had seen before.

His saddle 'twas a southern kack built many years ago,
　An O. K. spur on one foot idly hung,　　　[hind
While his "hot roll" in a cotton sack was loosely tied be-
　And a canteen from the saddle horn he'd slung.

He said he'd had to leave his home, his daddy'd married
　　　twice
　And his new ma beat him every day or two;
So he saddled up old Chaw one night and "Lit a shuck"
　　　this way
　Thought he'd try and paddle now his own canoe.

Said he'd try and do the best he could if we'd only give
　　　him work
　Though he didn't know "straight" up about a cow,
So the boss he cut him out a mount and kinder put him on
　For he sorter liked the little stray somehow.

Taught him how to herd the horses and to learn to know
    them all
  To round'em up by daylight; if he could
To follow the chuck-wagon and to always hitch the team
  And help the "cosinero" rustle wood.

We'd driven to red river and the weather had been fine;
  We were camped down on the south side in a bend
When a norther commenced blowing and we doubled up
    our guards
  For it took all hands to hold the cattle then.

Little Joe the wrangler was called out with the rest
  And scarcely had the kid got to the herd
When the cattle they stampeded; like a hail storm, long
    they flew
  And all of us were riding for the lead.

'Tween the streaks of lightning we could see a horse far
    out ahead
  'Twas little Joe the wrangler in the lead;
He was riding "old Blue Rocket" with his slicker 'bove
    his head
  Trying to check the leaders in their speed.

At last we got them milling and kinder quieted down
  And the extra guard back to the camp did go
But one of them was missin' and we all knew at a glance
  'Twas our little Texas stray poor wrangler Joe.

Next morning just at sunup we found where Rocket fell
   Down in a washout twenty feet below
Beneath his horse mashed to a pulp his horse had rung
   the knell
   For our little Texas stray—poor wrangler Joe.

Windy Bill

Windy Bill was a Texas man
     And he could rope you bet,
Talk of the steer he could'nt tie down
     Had'nt sort'er been born yet;
The boys they knew of an old black steer
     A sort of an old outlaw,
Who ran down in the bottom
     Just at the foot of the draw.

This slim black steer had stood his ground
     With punchers from everywhere
The boys bet Bill two to one
     He couldn't quite get there
So Bill brought up his old cow horse
     His weathers and back were sore
Prepared to tackle this old black steer
     Who ran down in the draw.

With his grazin' bits and sand stacked tree,
     His chaps and taps to boot,
His old maguey tied hard and fast,
     Went out to tackle the brute.

Bill sorter sauntered around him first;
    The steer began to paw
Poked up his tail high in the air
    And lit down in the draw.

The old cow horse flew at him like
    He'd been eatin' corn
And Bill he landed his old maguey
    Around old blackies horns.
The old time cow horse he stopped dead still,
    The cinches broke like straw
Both the sand stacked tree and old maguey,
    Went driftin' down the draw.

Bill landed in a big rock pile
    His face and hands were scratched;
He 'lowed he always could tie a steer
    But guessed he'd found his match.
Paid up his bet like a little man
    Without a bit of jaw
And said old blackie was the boss
    Of all down in the draw.

There's a moral to my song, boys,
    Which I hope that you can see
Whenever you start to tackle a steer
    Never tie hard your maguey.
Put on your dalebueltas
    'Cordin' to California law
And you will never see your old rim-fires
    Driftin' down the draw.

"The Tenderfoot"

I thought one spring just for fun
I'd see how cow-punching was done
So before the roundup was begun
  I tackled a cattle king.

Said he "my boss is down in town
He's at the Palace, his name is Brown;
I think to the ranch he'll take you down."
  "That's what I want," says I

We started to the ranch next day
Brown augered me most all the way
Told me cow-punching was just child's play
  It was no work at all.

For all you have to do is ride
Its only drifting with the tide
Oh how that old cow puncher lied
  He surely had his gall.

He saddled me up an old gray hack
With three set-fasts upon his back
Then padded him up with gunny sacks
  And used my bedding all.

Put me in charge of the Caballada
And told me not to work too hard
For all I had to do was ride
  And keep the horses near.

I had one hundred and sixty head
Sometimes I wished that I were dead
Brown's head would often get bright red
   If any got away.

Straight to the bushes they would take
As if they were running for a stake
I've often wished their necks they'd break
   But they would never fall.

Sometimes I couldn't head them all
At other times my horse would fall
And I'd roll on like a cannon ball
   Till earth got in my way.

When I got on he gave a bound
Sprung in the air and turned around
Just then my head hit on the ground
   It was an awful fall.

He picked me up and carried me in
He bathed my head and commenced to grin
Says that's the way they all begin
   You're doing very well.

To-morrow morning if you don't croak
I'll give you another horse that's broke
You'll not need a saddle or even a rope
   "No, I'll quit right here," says I.

"California Trail."

❦ ❦ ❦

List all you Californ'y boys
   And open wide your ears
For now we start across the plains
   With a herd of mules and steers.
Now bear it in mind before you start
   That you'll eat jerked beef not ham
And antelope steak oh cuss the stuff
   It often proves a sham.

You cannot find a stick of wood
   On all this prairie wide
Whene'er you eat you've got to stand
   Or sit on some old bull hide.
It's fun to cook with Buffalo Chips
   Or Mesquite green as corn
If I'd once known what I know now
   I'd have gone around Cape Horn.

The women have the hardest time
   Who emigrate by land
For when they cook out in the wind
   They're sure to burn their hands.
Then they scold their husbands 'round
   Get mad and spill the tea
I'd have thanked my stars if they'd not come out
   Upon this bleak prairie.

Most every night we put out guards
    To keep the Indians off
When night comes round some heads will ache
    And some begin to cough.
To be deprived of help at night
    You know it's mighty hard
But every night there's someone sick
    To get rid of standing guard.

Then they're always talking of what they've got
    And what they're going to do
Some will say they are content
    For I've got as much as you.
Others will say I'll buy or sell
    And damned if I care which
Others will say boy's buy him out
    For he doesn't own a stitch.

Old rawhide shoes are Hell on corns
    While tramping through the sands
And driving a Jackass by the tail
    Damn the overland.
I would as lief be on a raft at sea
    And there at once be lost
John let's leave this poor old mule
    We'll never get him across.

"Top Hand"

❦ ❦ ❦

While you're all so frisky I'll sing a little song
Think a horn of whiskey will help the thing along
It's all about the Top Hand when he's busted flat
Bumming round town, in his Mexican hat
He'd laid up all winter and his pocket book is flat
His clothes are all tatters but he don't mind that.

See him in town with a crowd that he knows
Rolling cigarettes an' a smoking through his nose.
First thing he tells you, he owns a certain brand
Leads you to think he is a daisy hand
Next thing he tells you 'bout his trip up the trail
All the way to Kansas to finish out his tale.

Put him on a horse, he's a handy hand to work
Put him on the branding pen he's dead sure to shirk.
With his natural leaf tobacco in the pockets of his vest
He'll tell you his Californy pants are the best.
He's handled lots of cattle, has'nt any fears
Can draw his sixty dollars, for the balance of his years.

Put him on herd, he's a cussin all day
Anything tries, its sure to get away.
When you have a round up he tells it all about
He's going to do the cuttin' and you can't keep him out.
If anything goes wrong he lays it on the screws
Say's the lazy devils were trying to take a snooze.

When he meets a greener he aint afraid to rig
Stands him on a chuck box and makes him dance a jig.
Waives a loaded cutter, makes him sing and shout,
He's a regular Ben Thompson, when the boss aint about.
When the boss aint about he leaves his leggins in camp.
He swears a man who wears them is worse than a tramp.

Say's he's not caring for the wages that he earns
For Dad's rich in Texas 'n got wagon loads to burn
But when he goes to town he's sure to take it in
He's always been dreaded, wherever he has been.
He rides a fancy horse, he is a favorite man
Can get more credit than a common waddie can.

When you ship the cattle he's bound to go along
To keep the boss from drinking and to see that nothing's
Wherever he goes, catch on to his game   [wrong
He likes to be called with a handle to his name.
He's always primping with a pocket looking glass
From the top to the bottom he's a bold Jackass.
           Waddie Cow boy.

Grand Round-up."

❦ ❦ ❦

(Repeat last two lines of each stanza.)
Air Bonnie Lies Over the Ocean

I hear there's to be a grand round up
   Where cow-boys with others must stand
To be cut out by the riders of judgment
   Who are posted and know all the brands.

The trail to that great mystic region
   Is narrow and dim so they say
While the one that leads down to perdition
   Is posted and blazed all the way.

Whose fault is it then that so many
   Go astray on this wild range and fail
Who might have been rich and had plenty
   Had they known of the dim narrow trail.

I wonder if at the last day some cow-boy
   Un-branded and un-claimed should stand
Would he be mavericked by those riders of judgment
   Who are posted and know all the brands?

My wish for all cow-boys is this
   That we may meet at that grand final sale
Be cut out by the riders of judgment
   And shoved up the dim narrow trail.

"Little Adobe Casa"

Just one year ago to-day,
   I left my eastern home
Hunting for a fortune and for fame,
   Little did I think that now,
   I'd be in Mexico
In this little adóbe casa on the plains.

Chorus.

   The roof is ocateo,
   The coyotes far and near
The Greaser roams about the place all day
   Centipedes and Tarantulas
   Crawl o'er me while I sleep
In my little adóbe casa on the plains.

   Alacranies on the ceiling,
   Cockroaches on the wall.
My bill-of-fare is always just the same
   Frijoles and tortillas
   Stirred up in chili sauce
In my little adóbe casa on the plains.

   But if some dark eyed mujer
   Would consent to be my wife
I would try to be contented and remain
   'Till fate should show a better place
   To settle down for life
Than this little adóbe casa on the plains.

The Texas Cow-boy.

Come all you Texas cow-boys
  And warning take of me
Don't go out in Montana
  For wealth or liberty
But stay home here in Texas
  Where they work the year around
And where you'll not get consumption
  From sleeping on the ground.

Montana is too cold for me,
  And the winters are too long
Before the round-ups have begun,
  Your money is all gone
For in Montana the boys get work
  But six months in the year
And they charge for things three prices
  In that land so bleak and drear.

This thin old hen-skin bedding
  'Twas not enough to shield my form
For I almost freeze to death,
  Whene'er there comes a storm.
I've an outfit on the Mussleshell
  Which I expect I'll never see
Unless by chance I'm sent
  To represent this A R and P T.

All along these bad lands,
    And down upon the dry
Where the cañons have no bottoms
    And the mountains reach the sky
Your chuck is bread and bacon
    And coffee black as ink
And hard old alkali water
    Thats scarcely fit to drink.

They'll wake you in the morning
    Before the break of day
And send you out on circle,
    Full twenty miles away.
With a "Tenderfoot" to lead you
    Who never knows the way
You're pegging in the best of luck
    If you get two meals a day.

I've been over in Colorado
    And down upon the Platte
Where the cow-boys work in pastures
    And the cattle all are fat
Where they ride silver mounted saddles
    And spurs and leggin's too
And their horses are all Normans
    And only fit to plow.

Yes I've traveled lots of country,
   Arizona's hills of sand
Down through the Indian Nation
   Plum to the Rio Grande
Montana is the bad-land
   The worst I've ever seen
Where the cow-boys are all tenderfeet
   And the dogies are all lean.

"Mustang Gray."

There was a brave old Texan
   They called him Mustang Gray
He left his home when quite a boy
   And went roaming far away.

Chorus.

He'll go no more a-rangering
   Those savages to affright
He has heard his last war-whoop
   He fought his last fight.

When our country was invaded
   By the Indian warriors train's
He used to mount his noble charger
   And scout the hills and plains.

He would not sleep within a tent
  No pleasures did he know
But like a brave old frontiersman
  A-scouting he would go.

Once he was taken prisoner
  And carried far away
Had to wear the yoke of bondage
  Through the streets of Monterey.

A señorita loved him
  And with a brave woman's pride
She opened the gates and gave him
  Her father's horse to ride.

And when this gallant life was spent
  This was his last command
Pray bury me in old Texas soil
  On the banks of the Rio Grande.

And when the weary treveller
  Is passing by his grave
He may sometimes shed a farewell tear
  O'er the bravest of the brave.

Sam Bass

Sam Bass was born in Indiana, it was his native home
And at the age of seventeen, young Sam began to roam
He first went down to Texas, a cow-boy bold to be
A kinder hearted fellow, you'd scarcely ever see.

Sam used to deal in race stock, had one called the Den-
  ton mare
He watched her in scrub races, took her to the County
  Fair.
She always won the money, wherever she might be
He always drank good liquor, and spent his money free.

Sam left the Collins ranch in the merry month of May
With a herd of Texas cattle the B'ack Hills to see
Sold out in Custer City and all got on a spree
A harder lot of cow-boys you'd scarcely ever see.

On the way back to Texas, they robbed the U. P. train
All split up in couples and started out again
Joe Collins and his partner were overtaken soon
With all their hard earned money they had to meet their
  doom.
Sam made it back to Texas all right side up with care
Rode into the town of Denton his gold with friends to
  share
Sam's life was short in Texas 'count of robberies he'd do
He'd rob the passengers coaches the mail and express too

Sam had four bold companions, four bold and daring lads
Underwood and Joe Jackson, Bill Collins and Old Dad
They were four of the hardest cow-boys that Texas ever
  knew
They whipped the Texas Rangers and ran the hoys in
  blue.

Jonis borrowed of Sam's money and didn't want to pay
The only way he saw to win was to give poor Sam away
He turned traitor to his comrades they were caught one
    early morn
Oh what a scorching Jonis will get whem Gabriel blows
    his horn.

Sam met his fate in Round Rock July the twenty-first
They pierced poor Sam with rifle balls and emptied out
    his purse
So Sam is a corpse in Round Rock, Jonis is under the clay
And Joe Jackson in the bushes trying to get away.

Bucking Broncho

My love is a rider, wild bronchos he breaks
Though he's promised to quit it, just for my sake
He ties up one foot, the saddle puts on
With a swing and a jump he is mounted and gone.

The first time I met him, 'twas early one spring
Riding a broncho a high headed thing
He tipped me a wink as he gaily did go
For he wished me to look at his bucking broncho.

The next time I saw him, 'twas late in the fall
Swinging the girls at Tomlinson's ball
He laughed and he talked, as we danced to and fro
Promised never to ride on another broncho.

He made me some presents, among them a ring
The return that I made him was a far better thing
'Twas a young maiden's heart, I'd have you all know
He'd won it by riding his bucking broncho.

Now all you young maidens, where'er you reside
Beware of the cow-boy who swings the rawhide
He'll court you and pet you and leave you and go
In the spring up the trail on his bucking broncho.

Educated Feller

We were camped upon the plains near the Cimmaron
When along came a stranger and stopped to argue some
He was a well educated feller his talk just come in herds
And astonished all the punchers with his jaw breaking
    words.

He had a well worn saddle and we thought it kind'er
    strange
That he didn't know much about working on the range
He'd been at work he said, up near the Santa Fe
And was cutting cross country to strike the 7 D.

Had to quit an outfit up near Santa Fe
Had some trouble with the boss, just what he didn't say
Said his horse was 'bout give out would like to get
    another
If the punchers wouldn't mind and it wasn't too much
    bother.

Yes we'll give you a horse, he's just as sound as a bun
They quickly grabbed a lariat and roped the Zebra Dun.
Turned him over to the stranger
Then they waited to see the fun.

Old Dunny stands right still not seeming to know
Until the strangers' ready and a fixing up to go
When he goes into the saddle old Dunny leaves the earth
He travels right straight up for all he was worth.

But he sits up in his saddle just pullin his mustach
Just like some summer boarder a waitin for his hash
Old Dunny pitched and bauled and had wall eyed fits
His hind feet perpendicular his front ones in his bits.

With one foot in the stirupp, he just thought it fun
The other leg around the saddle horn the way he rode
      old Dun.
He spurred him in the shoulder and hit him as he whirled
Just to show these flunky punchers the best rider in the
      world.

The boss says to him, you needn't go on
If you can use the rope like you rode old Dun.
You've a job with me if you want to come
You're the man I've been looking for since the year one.

I can sling the rope, an' I'm not very slow
I can catch nine times out of ten for any kind of dough

Now there's one thing and a sure thing I've learned
    since I was born
That all these educated fellows are not green horns.

Cow Boys Lament.

'Twas once in my saddle I used to be happy
    'Twas once in my saddle I used to be gay
But I first took to drinking, then to gambling
    A shot from a six-shooter took my life away.

My curse let it rest, let it rest on the fair one
    Who drove me from friends that I loved and from home
Who told me she loved me, just to deceive me
    My curse rest upon her, wherever she roam.

Oh she was fair, Oh she was lovely
    The belle of the Viliage the fairest of all
But her heart was as cold as the snow on the mountains
    She gave me up for the glitter of gold.

I arrived in Galveston in old Texas
    Drinking and gambling I went to give o'er
But, I met with a Greaser and my life he has finished
    Home and relations I ne'er shall see more.

Send for my father, Oh send for mother
    Send for the surgeon to look at my wounds
But I fear it is useless I feel I am dying
    I'm a young cow-boy cut down in my bloom.

Farewell my friends, farewell my relations
   My earthly career has cost me sore
The cow-boy ceased talking, they knew he was dying
   His trials on earth, forever were o'er.

Chor· Beat your drums lightly, play your fifes merrily
   Sing your dearth march as you bear me along
Take me to the grave yard, lay the sod o'er me
   I'm a young cow-boy and know I've done wrong.

Chopo.

Through rocky arroyas so dark and so deep
Down the sides of the mountains so slippery and steep
You've good judgment, sure footed, wherever you go
You're a safety conveyance my little Chopo

Whether single or double or in the lead of a team
Over highways or byways or crossing a stream
You're always in fix and willing to go
Whenever you're called on, my chico Chopo.

You're a good roping horse, you were never jerked down
When tied to a steer, you will circle him round
Let him once cross the string, and over he'll go
You sabe the business, my cow horse Chopo.

One day on the Llano, a hail storm began
The herds were stampeded, the horses all ran
The lightning it glittered, a cyclone did blow
But you faced the sweet music my little Chopo.

Chopo my pony, Chopo my pride
Chopo my amigo, Chopo I will ride
From Mexico's borders 'cross Texas Llanos
To the salt Pecos river I ride you Chopo.

Buffalo Range.

Come all you Buffalo hunters and listen to my song
You needn't get uneasy, for it isn't very long
It's concerning some Buffalo hunters who all agreed to go
And spend a summer working, among the buffalo.

'Twas in the spring of seventy three, that I came to
    Jacksborough
There I met Bailey Griego, who asked how I'd like to go
And spend the summer west of Pease River hunting
On the range of the Buffalo.

Now being out of employment to Griego I named the
    day
When I could join his outfit if suited with the pay
I agreed if he'd pay good wages and transportation to,
To go and spend the summer among the buffalo.

Of course I'll pay good wages and transportation to
But if you should grow homesick and return to Jacksbor-
    ough
Before the huntings over I want you now to know
That I'll not pay you back wages from the range of the
    Buffalo.

Through promises and flattery he enlisted quite a train
Some ten or twelve in number all able bodied men
Our journey it was pleanant on the road we had to go
Until we crossed Pease River among the buffalo.

'Twas here our pleasure ended, our troubles had begun
The very first beast I tried to skin Oh how I cut my
   thumb
When skinning off those buffalo hides for our lives we'd
   little show
As the Indians tried to pick us off on the range of the
   buffalo.

Salt meat and Buffalo hump to eat and hard old sour
   dough bread
Strong coffee and alkali water to drink add a raw-hide
   for a bed
The way the mosquitos chewed on us you bet it wasn't
   slow
Lord grant there's no place on earth like the range of
   the buffalo.

When the summer at last ended old Griego began to say
My boys you've been extravagant, so I'm in debt to day
But among the buffalo hunters bankrupt law didn't go
So we left old Griegos bones to bleach among the buffalo.

Now we're back across Peace River and homeward we
   are bound
In that forsaken country may I never more be found

If you see anyone bound out there pray warn them not
     to go
To that forsaken country, the land of the buffalo.

The Cowboys Christmas Ball

Way out in Western Texas where the Clear Forks wa-
     ters flow
Where the cattle are a brewin' and the Spanish ponies
     grew
Where the Northers come a whistlin' from beyond the
     Neutral Strip
And the prairie dogs are sneezin' as though they had
     the grip
Where the coyotes come a-howlin' round the ranches af-
     ter dark
And the mocking-birds are singin' to the lovely Medder
     Lark
Where the possum and the badger and the rattlesnakes
     abound
And the monstrous stars are winkin' o'er a wilderness
     prefound
Where lonesome tawney prairies melt into air'y streems
While the Double Mountains slumber in heaven'ly kinds
     of dreams
Where the Antelope is grazin' and the lonely plovers call
It was there that I attended The Cowboys Christmas
     Ball.

The town was Anson City—old Jones' County Seat
Where they raised Poled Angus cattle and waving
    whiskered wheat
Where the air is soft and balmy and dry and full of health
And the prairies is exploding with Agricultural wealth
Where they print the ''Texas Western'' that Hue Mc-
    Call supplies
With news and yarns and stories of most amazin' size
Where Frank Smith ''pulls the badger'' on knowin' ten-
    derfeet
And Democracy's triumphant and mighty hard to bea'
Where lives that good old hunter John Milsap from La
    mar
Who used to be the sheriff ''back east in Paris sah''
'Twas there I say at Ansen with the lovely widder Wal
That I went to that reception The Cowboys Christmas
    Ball.
The boys had left the ranches and come to town in piles
The ladies kinder' scatterin' had gathered in for miles
And yet the place was crowded as I remember well
'Twas gave on this occasion at the Morning Star Hotel
The music was a fiddle and a lively tambeurine
And a ''Viol'' came imported by the stage from Abilene
The room was togged out gorgeous with Mistletoe and
    shawls
And the candles flickered festious around the airy walls
The women folks looked lovely the boys looks kinder
    treed

'Till the leader commenced yellin' "whoa   fellers   lets
    stampede"
And the music started sighin' and a wailin' through the
    hall
As a kind of introduction to ·"The Cowboys Christmas
    Ball".

The leader was a feller that came from Tomsons ranch
They called him "Windy Billy" from little Deadmans
    branch
His rig was kinder keerless big spurs and high heeled
    boots
He had the reputation that comes when fellers shoots
His voice was like a bugle upon the Mountains height
His feet were animated and a mighty moving sight
When he commenced to holler"'now fellers stake yer pen"
Lock horns ter all them heifers and russle them like men
Saloot yer lovely critters neow swing and let'em go
Climb the grape vine round'em all hands do-ce-do
You Mavericke jine the round-up jest skip the water fall
Auh hit was gettin' active"The Cowboys Christmas Ball.

The boys were tolerable skittish the ladies powerful neat
That old bass Viols music just got there with both feet
That wailin' frisky fiddler I never shall forget
And Windy kept singin' I think I hear him yet
O'Yes Chase your Squirrels and cut'em to our side
Spur Treadwell to the centre with Cress P Charlie's
    bride

Doc' Hollis down the middle and twice the ladies chain
Van Andrews pen the fillies in big T Diamonds train
All pull your freight together neow swallow fork an
    change
Big Boston lead the trail herd through little Pitchfork's
    range
Purr round yor gentle pussies neow rope'em balance all
Huh hit was gettin' active "The Cowboys Christmas Ball

The dust riz fast and furious we all just galloped round
Till the scenery got so giddy that T Bar Dick wes down'd
We buckled to our partners an' told'em to hold on
Then shook our hoofs like lightning until the early dawn
Don't tell me 'bout Cotillions or Germans No Sir 'Ee
That whirl at Anson City just takes the cake with me
I'm sick of lazy shufflings of them I've had my fill
Give me a frontier break-down backed up by Windy Bill
McAllister aint nowhere when Windy leads the show
I've seen 'em both in harness and so I sorter know
Oh Bill I shant forget you I'll oftentimes recall
That lively gaited sworray"The Cowboys Christmas Ball

Chase of the O. L. C. Steer

Did you ever hear of the O L C Steer
    With widely flaring horns
He smashes the trees as he splits the breeze
    And the Cow-boys ropes he scorns

That O L C's fame it soon became
  Of camp fire yarns the pet
I'll stake my rocks that I get that ox
  Quoth Rap Who'll take my bet?

Why of course my Gray Black horse
  Will run on him he said
Show me his track I'll bring him back
  I'll bet alive or dead.

Up Johnny spoke "No brags I make"
  Straight goods I give you now
I'll put my string on anything
  From a coyote to a cow.

Then up spoke Bob with this here job
  You bet I'm going to cope
Just you watch me if you want to see
  How Texas punchers rope.

These cow-boys three for modesty
  Have always been well known
For don't you know unless they blow
  Their horns they'd not be blown.

Meanwhile the steer devoid of fear
  Was trailing o'er the Mesa
He sniffed the air what did he care
  He knew he was a racer.

With firm intent on business bent
  Three youths rode up the trail

The steer he saw droppped his jaw
  And then he whisked his tail.

The other day I chanced that way
  That steer was grinning yet
Six weeks have passed not yet the last
  Of why that steer they didn't get.

If they once began for yours they'll chin
  And tell although they hit him
And ran all day how he got away
  And why they didn't git im''

The Pecos Stream

A cowboys life is a weary dreary life
  Some people think it free from all care
Its rounding up cattle from morning to night
  On the lone prairie so drear.

When the spring work comes in then our troubles begin
  The weather being fierce and cold
We get almose froze with the water on our clothes
  And the cattle we can scarcely hold.

Just about four o'clock the cook will holler out
  "Roll out boys its almost day"
Through his broken slumbers the puncher he will ask
  Has the short summer night passed away.

"Saddle up" "Saddle Up" the boss will holler out
  When we're camped by the Pecos stream
Where the wolves and the owls with their terrifying
      howls
  Disturb us in our midnight dreams.

Once I loved to roam but now I stay at home
  All you punchers take my advice
Sell your briddle and your saddle quit your roaming and
      travels
  And tie on to a cross eyed wife.

The Pecos River Queen.

Where the Pecos river winds and turns in its journey to
      the sea
From its white walls of sand and rock striving ever to
      be free
Near the highest railroad bridge that all these modern
      times have
Dwells fair young Patty Moorhead the Pecos River Queen

She's known by all the cowboys on the Pecos river wide
They know full well that she can shoot that she can rope
      and ride
She goes to every roundup every cow work without fail
Looking out for all Her Cattle branded "walking hog oh
      rail."
She made her start in cattle, yes, made it with her rope
Can tie down ev'ry maverick fore it can strike a lope

She can rope and tie and brand it as quick as any man
She's voted by all cowboys an A l top cow hand.

Across the Comstock Railroad bridge the highest in the
    west
Patty rode her horse one day a lovers heart to test
For he told her he would gladly risk all dangers for her
    sake
But the puncher wouldn't follow so she's still without a
    mate.

Old Time Cowboy

Come all you melancholy folks wherever you may be
I'll sing you about the cowboy whose life is light and free
He roams about the prairie and at night when he lies
    down
His heart is as gay as the flowers in May in his bed upon
    the ground.

They're a little bit rough I must confess the most of them
    at least
But if you do not hunt a quarrel you can live with them
    in peace
For if you do your sure to rue the day you joined their
    band
They will follow you up and shoot it out with you just
    man to man.

Did you ever go to any cowboy whenever hungry or dry
Asking for a dollar and have him you deny
He'll just pull out his pocket book and hand you a note
They are the fellows to help you out whenever you are
    broke.

Go to their ranches and stay awhile they never ask a cent
And when they go to town their money is freely spent
They walk straight up and take a drink paying for
    everyone
And they never ask your pardon for anything they have
    done

When they go to their dances some dance while others
    pat
They ride their bucking broncos and wear their broad
    brimmed hats
With their California saddles and their pants inside their
    boots
You can hear their spurs a-jingling and perhaps some of
    them shoot.

Come all softhearted tenderfeet if you want to have
    some fun
Go live among the cowboys they show you how it's done
They'll treat you like a prince my boys about them there's
    nothing mean
But dont try to give them too much advice for all of 'em
    aint so green.

Who's Old Cow

✺ ✺

Twas the end of roundup the last day of June
 Or maybe July I dont just remember
Or it might have been August 'twas some time ago
 Or perhaps 'twas the first of September.

Anyhow 'twas the roundup we had at Mayou
 On the lightning rod's range near Cayo
There was some twenty wagons ''more or less'' camped
  about
 On the temporal in the Cañon.

First night we'd no cattle so we only stood guard
 On the horses somewhere 'bout two hundred head
So we side-lined and hoppled we belled and we staked
 Loose'd our hot rolls and fell into bed.

Next morning 'bout daybreak we started our work
 Our horses like possums felt fine
Each ''one 'tendin' knitten!'' none trying to shirk
 So the roundup got on in good time.

Well we worked for a week 'till the country was clear
An' the boss said ''now boys we'll stay here
We'll carve and we'll trim 'em an' start out a herd
Up the east trail from old Abilene.

Next morning' all on herd an' but two with the cut
An' the boss on Piute carving fine

'Till he rode down his horse and had to pull out
An' a new man went in to clean up.

Well after each outfit had worked on the band
There was only three head of them left
When Nig Add from L F D outfit road in
A dictionary on earmarks an' brands.

He cut the two head out told where they belonged
But when the last cow stood there alone
Add's eyes bulged so he did'nt 'no just what to say
'Ceptin boss der's sumpin' here monstrous wrong.

White folks smarter'n Add an' maybe I'se wrong
But here's six months wages dat I'll give
If anyone'll tell me when I reads de mark
To who dis long horned cow belongs.

Overslope in right ear an' de underbill
Left ear swallerfork an de undercrop
Hole punched in centre an' de jinglebob
Under half crop an' de slash an split.

She's got O block an' lightnin' rod
Nine forty-six an' A bar eleven
T terrapin an' ninety-seven
Rafter cross an' de double prod.

Half circle A an' diamond D
Four cross L an' three P Z
B W I bar X V V
Bar N cross an' A L C

So if no' o' you punchers claims dis cow
Mr Stock 'Sociation need'nt get alarmed
For one brand more or less wont do no harm
So old nigger Add'l just brand her now

The Cowboys New Years Dance.

BY MARK CHISHOLM

We were sitting' round the ranch house some twenty
    hands or more
Most of us Americans but a few from Arkansas
One Dutchman from the fatherland one Johnny Bull
    from Leeds
A Cornishman from Cornwall all men of different creeds
They were a sittin' an' a arguin' busy as a hill of ants
How they'd get rid of the money they had buried in their
    pants
That they'd made by hard cow punching working all
    the year around
From sunup until sundown an' a sleepin' on the ground
Where at night the polecat saunters round the chuck box
    after grub
And in passing by your hot roll gives your head a friend-
    ly rub
Where the rattlesnake lays dormant his fangs are like
    a lance
'Twas with them that I attended The Cowboys New
    Years Dance.

The town was Roswell City old Chaves' county seat
Where they raise fine shorthorn cattle that are mighty
     hard to beat
Where they send the frail consumptive in search of in-
     stant health
And the hills is just a bustin' with their pent up mineral
     wealth
Where the wells are all artesian and fiow fish and water
     too
'Least so says the Roswell people so I sorter guess it's
     true
Where laughin' Joe the darky bust up Mulkey's show
     one day
By laughin' at prayer meetin' and old Abe he went away
Charles Perry he was a sheriff and G Curry county clerk
Where they caught Bill Cook the outlaw and sent him
     off to work
Where the moonbeams on the Pecos seem to glitter and
     to glance
I received an invitation to the Cowboys New Years
     Dance.

The boys had been invited and they just come in herds
The ladies more numerous had flocked to town like birds
Old Roswell was just crowded there was horses every-
     where

Looked like some long procession headed for a county fair
Where everything was orderly as I remember well
Invitations were extended to the Roswell Stone Hotel
The music was a fiddle a guitar and a banjo
And the way those three boys played em'
It was fully half the show the women folks set together
All the boys stood in the door 'tlll the caller commenced
    yellin'
For just one couple more
And the music started windin 'an' a wailin' like some
    hants
That had come to cast their hoodo on the Cowboy New
    Years Dance.

The caller was a feller one of Atkinson's men
Who had the reputation of once being in the pen
His outfit sort of gaudy big spurs an' conchas bright
Fringed leggin's and gold buttons six feet about his
    height
He was tall an' angular an, a broncho buster right
An' at callin' out the dances he was simply out of sight
Soon he commenced to beller now fellers all begin
Grab your lovely partners an' every one jine in
First bow to your partners now four hands cross an'
    change
An' chase those pretty footies once around the range
Join once again your partners around the circles prance
It was getting interesting the Cowboys New Years
    Dance,

Next dance will be the Lancers round up your ladies boys
Cut them all to the centre and never mind the noise
Chase your lovely critters all into the branding pen
Everybody swing everybody else's girl and swing them
      once again
Dash your line on the nearest filly and drag her from
      the herd
Re-sume your former places and swing her like a bird
Now Brownfield strike out in the lead all grand right
      and left
Swing each one when half way round never mind their
      hat
Now ladies to the centre all hands do se do
Right hand in left hand out swing and let her go
Trail block Jack to your settees for that winds up the
      lance
My but it was getting furious the Cowboys New Years
      Dance.

The refreshments came round often till all hands had
      their fill
Past round uncerimonous like by Broncho Buster Bill
Though his gait was quite uncertain he never lost his feet
And at complementing ladies he was mighty hard to beat
To close up the night proceedings we ragged "Turkey in
      the Straw"
Till we wore out musicians and they could play no more
We were served with soda water red eye and pilsner

beer

And the conversation never lagged 'twas most penetrat-
    ing clear

'En those who never danced before would dance with all
    their might

'En the most peaceably inclined citizens went a hunting
    for a fight

So we saddled up our horses drifted homeward to the
    ranch

With a happy recollection of the Cowboys New Years
    Dance.

Speckles

He was little 'en peaked 'en thin 'en Narr'y a no 'account
    horse

Least that's the way you'd describe him in case that the
    beast had been lost

But for single and double cussedness 'en double fired sin

The horse never come out O' Texas that was half way
    knee-high to him

The first time that ever I saw him was nineteen year ago
    last spring

'Twas the year we had grasshoppers that come 'en 'et
    up everything

That a feller rode up here one evening 'en wanted to pen
    overnight

A small bunch of horses he said 'en I told him I guessed
    'twas all right,

Well the feller was busted the horses was thin 'en the
    grass around here kind of good
'En he said if I'd let him hold here a few days He'd set-
    tle with me when he could
So I told him all right turn them lo⁻se down the draw
That the latch string was always untied
He was welcome to stop a few days if he liked 'En rest
    from his weary ride.

Well the cus stay'd around for two or three weeks till
    at last he decided to go
And that horse away yonder being too poor to move He
    gimme, the cuss had no dough
Well at first the darn brute was as wild as a deer 'en
    would snort when he came to the branch
'En it took two cowpunchers on good horses too to han-
    dle him here at the ranch

Well winter came on and the range it got hard and my
    mustang commenced to get thin
So I fed him along and rode him round some and found
    out old Freckles was game
For that was what the other cus called him just Freckles
    no more or no less
His color couldn't describe it something like a paintshop
    in distress.

Them was Indian times young feller that I'm a tellin'
    about
And oft's the time I've seen the red men fight and put
    the boys in blue to route
A good horse in them days young feller would save your
    life
One that in any race could hold the pace when the red-
    skin bands were rife.

APPLEWOOD BOOKS
BRINGING THE PAST ALIVE

TIMELESS ADVICE & ENTERTAINMENT
FROM AMERICANS WHO CAME BEFORE US

George Washington on Manners
Benjamin Franklin on Money
Lydia Maria Child on Raising Children
Henry David Thoreau on Walking

&

Many More Distinctive Classics
Now Available Again

At finer bookstores
& gift shops or from:

APPLEWOOD BOOKS
18 North Road
Bedford, MA 01730